I AM HER

Create The Life You Love & Follow Your Heart

Written By Krystal Zayas Figueroa

A SELF-DEVELOPMENT JOURNAL TO BE ALL GOD CALLED YOU TO BE

All rights reserved. No part of this book may be reproduced or transmitted in any form or by any means without written permission from the author.

Scripture is noted from The Authorized (King James) Version. Rights in the Authorized Version in the United Kingdom are vested in the Crown. Reproduced by permission of the Crown's patentee, Cambridge University Press

Scriptures marked ESV are taken from the THE HOLY BIBLE, ENGLISH STANDARD VERSION (ESV): Scriptures taken from THE HOLY BIBLE, ENGLISH STANDARD VERSION ® Copyright© 2001 by Crossway, a publishing ministry of Good News Publishers. Used by permission.

Scripture quotations marked (NIV) are taken from the Holy Bible, New International Version®, NIV®. Copyright © 1973, 1978, 1984, 2011 by Biblica, Inc.™ Used by permission of Zondervan. All rights reserved worldwide. www.zondervan.com The "NIV" and "New International Version" are trademarks registered in the United States Patent and Trademark Office by Biblica, Inc.™

Scriptures marked NKJV are taken from the NEW KING JAMES VERSION (NKJV): Scripture taken from the NEW KING JAMES VERSION®. Copyright© 1982 by Thomas Nelson, Inc. Used by permission. All rights reserved.

I AM HER: Create The Life You Love & Follow Your Heart
Copyright © 2021 by Krystal Zayas Figueroa
Published By: You Can Make It Books, LLC
www.youcanmakeitbooks.com
ISBN: 978-1-7366651-3-8

Dedication

This book is dedicated to all the beautiful souls in the world. This is for you. It's never too late to dream big! Go after your dreams, trust in the Lord & follow your heart!

Acknowledgments

I would like to acknowledge the Lord above for all He has provided for me and my family thus far. It is because of Him that anything is possible. Thank you, Lord Father God, I do it all by your glory.

I would like to acknowledge my mother Linda who has been there for me every step of the way. Thank you for the way you raised me, you are my mother and father, and you are my role model. Thank you for always believing in my dreams, supporting me in every area of my life, and for always telling me to always go after my dreams. Your words always stay with me for the rest of my life, and I love you with all my heart and soul.

I would like to acknowledge my grandparents Josephine & Joseph (R.I.P), although you may not be here in the physical world, you will forever live in my heart. It was because of you papa and mama who told me since I was little; that I was going to become someone someday. Thank you for planting that seed into my life and loving me unconditionally.

I would like to acknowledge my husband Steven Oscar Figueroa, for always believing in me. Always seeing the potential in me, supporting my dreams, and always being there for me in my ups and my downs. Who always wants the best for me. Thank you so much, my love, it is because of you that I got to feel the love of God. Also to know how it truly feels to believe in myself. Thank you for loving me the same way the Lord loves the church. I love you, Babe.

I would like to acknowledge all of my former teachers from kindergarten, all the way through college. You've all made such a huge impact in my life. The reason why I continue to strive is due to the fact; that all of you choose to believe in my potential and never choose to give up on me. I will never forget what you all have done for me throughout the years. I am so thankful for each and every one of you.

I would like to acknowledge all of my friends in life. God put you in my life for a reason. I am so blessed to have each and every single one of you as a friend. Thank you for all that you do for me in my life.

I would like to acknowledge my family. To all of my siblings, thank you for all of your divine support and love. Showing me what the word "FAMILY" means. Family means the world to me and I love each and every single one of you.

I would like to acknowledge all of my in-laws. You all have made such a huge difference in my life. Thank you for loving me as your own, believing in me, and supporting me. I love you all so much.

I would like to acknowledge "You Can Make It Books LLC". Thank you so much for making my dream a reality.

INTRODUCTION

Welcome!

Hi beautiful souls! My name is Krystal, and I am so excited that this book is in your hands. I know you are ready for a one-of-a-kind journal experience. During our time together with each question, just write what comes from your heart as well as expressing your soul. Express yourself, no holding back.

I am a teacher, author, and a certified life coach. Helping those in need sets my soul on fire. It is who I am. I love to make a difference in someone's life, to make a difference in the world one day at a time. I know what it feels like to be lost, overwhelmed, depressed, and feel like the Lord is distant from you. I have been down in the dumps with no way out, but I never lost my faith. I never lost hope and most importantly, I stayed in prayer through it all. I saw that with every bad thing that happened in my life. There was a blessing in disguise. I asked myself "What was the Lord trying to teach me today?". Each experience I faced and battled, is what shaped me, and it helped me slowly get to where I am now. What the power of prayer can do, right?

I created this journal so you can look deep within yourself and find who you truly are. Sometimes we ask ourselves questions like "What is my purpose on this earth?". Am I listening to what the Lord is telling me? Am I following my heart or the crowd? Which path should I take? Is this for me? How is my mindset? Am I meeting my goals, or is there fear holding me back? Or is there anything in my life I need to see a breakthrough in? These questions that we ask ourselves, help us with our self-growth, mindset, and development.

Among the many questions that I ask in this journal, I pray that you receive peace and clarity that you"ve been longing for. I love you all! And thank you for starting here. So, let's get started, shall we?

The Bible tells us………..

Jeremiah 29:11 (NIV)

"For I know the plans I have for you, declares the LORD, plans for welfare and not for evil, to give you a future and a hope."

The Lord has your future for you, He knows all about you.

NEVER QUESTION YOUR WORTH!

Why must we compare ourselves to others? We see others and we wish we had the same color of hair, car, or house. But if that were the case, the Lord would make all of us identical right? But He didn't, we each have our own way of life. Each of us have different morals and beliefs and that's ok. It is ok to be different from one another, because being different, is how we are truly able to find ourselves. If everyone was exactly the same; then none of us would be able to discover on what makes us special. What sets us apart from all the rest. It is ok to be different.

My dear, what I am trying to tell you is: love the skin you're in. Love your culture, religion, heritage etc. All of this is what helps you identify as yourself. You were born to stand out and to make a difference in the world. You are not a copy, you are an original made by God. He doesn't make mistakes.

LOVE WHAT YOU SEE IN THE MIRROR

Lately, I had a thought and it's about how society makes us ladies feel so ugly. But why?

There's a reason why they spend millions of dollars on advertising and marketing strategies. To make you unsatisfied with your life and yourself. Sometimes we get so caught up in society's definition of beauty which is "Perfection", an unrealistic target that constantly moves. Truth is, it's the society that's ugly. Why do women feel as though they need to compete with other females on looks, style, husband, lifestyle etc? Aren't we all equal? We are supposed to be united, not divided. Aren't we all unique? No wonder we are so critical about ourselves when we look at the mirror. Questioning ourselves, asking, am I beautiful? Oh, but there's a pimple on my face that needs to go away. Do you know it takes 7-8 compliments to cancel out a criticizing comment? So, for the past week, I have been looking into the mirror and for once in my life, I didn't look for cracks in myself. I didn't look for my flaws or imperfections. I asked myself who is this girl? She is Krystal Ann. She is 5ft 3 of beauty and perfect just the way she is because God created her in His image. She loves to dance, write, teach, coach, paint, eat, spend time with family, and read. She is humble, clumsy, kind, loveable, organized, weird, and random. She is an empath. Now, if I were to compliment her, I'd say: "You have inspired me since you went through so much in your life girl, nothing can stop you. Keep on going! Keep believing in yourself, and most of all never give up.". Or perhaps "She has met a woman who is also going through what she went through; to be happy with who they are and be comfortable in their own skin." Or "She inspires girls to go out there and try to make a difference in the world." Or simple nice things about myself would be "She really cares for her mother, her family, and her husband and would do anything for them. She's exercising, and dancing again and keeping fit! You got it, girl!". I've never said this to myself before. I also started saying daily affirmations, mantras, and Bible verses which also helped me with my self-esteem. My self-love, happiness, and confidence. I've heard wonderful encouraging comments from wonderful people but, when you speak to yourself and really believe it. You will be truly amazed by how much compassion you will have, for the person that you see staring back at you in the mirror. When I look at the mirror, damn it, I love this girl! I'm going to take good care of her by encouraging her rather than putting her down. You are your own biggest fan. Love yourself for who you are, always!

So now when I look at the mirror, I see a loving girl looking back at me. With eyes that look for goodness in others and herself. Instead of looking for the small imperfections, my redness, wrinkles, and other flaws. Look beyond these external factors, because it's not about what's on the outside, but what's on the inside that really matters. (THE HEART ALWAYS REMEMBER THAT!).

Don't just think about it. SAY IT! There is power in your words and the more you say it out loud, the more your mind will believe it. "BE CONFIDENT, BE HAPPY, BE YOU". Most of all, "LOVE YOURSELF". I know from experience, love yourself first so that you can love others just as much.

What do you see when you look in the mirror? Do you love what is staring back at you? What will you say to yourself today?

NEVER GIVE UP

Negative thoughts will come into your mind.
It's up to you if you allow it to come in and to ruin you from the inside.
Work on yourself and train your mind to think positive thoughts, and say you rebuke the enemy in the name of Jesus.
Life is hard, no one said it will be easy. We have to live every day like if it's our last because tomorrow is never promised.
Most people give up
When they are very close
To the dreams and ambitions, thinking "wow I got this far," but the more you go the harder it gets. It's a test from God, keep going, and don't let the hardships stop you!

Never give up the fight
Whatever happens in life
Push forward, and NEVER GIVE UP!

Always believe in yourself, have confidence in all you do. Have hope and dream big. The people who love you will believe in you always. Who cares what people think of you, at the end of the day it's only what you think about yourself.

Do you care about what other people think about you? When was the last time someone told you something and it made you feel less confident?

In the Bible, here is what it says about not giving up, it says;

So do not fear, for I am with you; do not be dismayed, for I am your God. I will strengthen you and help you; I will uphold you, with My righteous right hand.

-Isaiah 41:10(NIV)

Being confident of this, that He who began a good work in you will carry it on to completion until the day of Christ Jesus.

-Philippians 1:6(NIV)

When Jesus spoke again to the people, He said, "I am the light of the world. Whoever follows me will never walk in darkness but will have the light of life."

- John 8:12(NIV)

Jesus looked at them and said, "With man this is impossible, but with God all things are possible."

-Mathew 9:26(NIV)

What is your definition of what true love is?

What does family mean to you?

MY TESTIMONY

Feb. 2015 was a day and the year to remember because it was when the Lord made me realize I was experiencing spiritual warfare. Yes, it does exist. There is good and evil out there, the same way there is a God (my Lord and Savior) there is the Devil. In that year, I was such a hateful person, and I would never hate anyone, that's not in my nature. I'm not that type to hate anyone. I am a very loving, humble, sweet, and genuine person. That year I wasn't myself, it was like I was a different person. I wasn't eating every day and when I tried to eat, I threw it right back up. I was losing weight. I was hearing negative voices in my head and had negative thoughts telling me to cut myself and to end my life. I've tried numerous times to do so but the last time when I tried to commit suicide I heard.

"Stop! I love you." After hearing that, it brought me comfort and a sense of peace I have never felt before. I would also hear the negative voice that said "You have no purpose, you're worthless, your ugly" which was making things so much worse because I believed in the lies. Now I know that the devil steals, lies, and cheats. In John 10:10 it says" The thief (devil) cometh not, but that he may steal, and kill and destroy I (the Lord) came that they may have life and have [it] abundantly." The Lord is the way to the truth. In 2 Thessalonians: 3 it says: " But the Lord is faithful, He will strengthen and protect you from the evil one."

The voices kept going on for months. It was getting worse and worse, until one night I said a prayer to the Lord (and I pray every single day). In my prayer, I said Lord, people are telling me this is spiritual warfare, and I know you are testing my love for you Lord…... I trust in you always and I know you won't leave my side…... please God give me a sign, In Jesus' name amen!". When I said that prayer, I had chills coming down my spine. That night when I fell asleep, I had a dream.

In that dream what I saw was pitch white, it was so white and beautiful. In the dream, I felt so much love, bliss, and harmony. When I looked forward there was heaven with a golden gate and a hand that reached out to me so I could go with Him. But as soon as I grabbed the hand which I knew was the Lord, I looked behind me and I saw a hideous creature. That had a body just like a human, but the head was shaped like a bull with horns, and I couldn't look at him. The creature was running after me with a gun in his hand trying to kill me and as I kept running (Just like how it is in the movies where the person keeps on running and it feels like an eternal where they will never reach their destination.). I kept on running and as soon as I was about to reach for the Lord's hand, the creature grabbed me by a chokehold, and I was crying saying please no! Please don't kill me! He shot me in my left leg but when I looked down at my leg the wound was starting to heal on its own. Then I woke up from that dream, with a bruise on my leg that was never there before. That same bruise was in the exact same location where I got shot in the dream. I also woke up in tears because of the fact that I was in disbelief of what happened. To me honestly, I was in total shock, that dream felt too real and to this day, I will never forget it.

  Then I heard a voice speak to me and instructed me to go to a certain page in the Bible. When I opened that page it said, "I am jealous of your relationship with God". I started to cry. Ever since that day, I've gotten the help I needed thanks to the love of my life and his family, my mother and grandmother, my family, the Lord, and especially with prayer. From that moment forward, I just knew that my life would begin to change for the better. I began to attend prayer meetings, at The Brooklyn Tabernacle church with my love and going to the healing masses each Tuesday at 7:00 pm. Where they would put their hand on you and pray over you. With those praying sessions, I've begun to notice a significant change in my life. Both mentally and spiritually. Here I am today, a changed person in Christ. My faith has gotten stronger than before, I preach to people about the good Lord because the Lord wants His children to know who he is and to follow Him. When we seek him wholeheartedly, our lives will really be transformed. In Romans 10:9,10,13 it says "If you confess with your mouth that Jesus is Lord and believe in your heart that God raised Him from the dead, you will be saved. For it is by believing in your heart that you are made right with God, and it is by confessing with your mouth that you are saved… For everyone who calls on the name of the Lord will be saved." If you let the Lord into your life, repent of your sins and He will wash away all your sins. You will be completely forgiven In God's eyes. I feel it was in my will to write this because in my heart I know God wants me to share my experiences with His children. Although not everyone may agree with me, God has the power to change lives around. No matter if you have your own beliefs; or if you have no beliefs at all. One last thing I would like to leave you with; is to understand that with God nothing is impossible for Him. He has the absolute power to make anything impossible become possible. God is good, God is love, and God is real!

What is your testimony? What has God taught you?

Right now, do you feel close to or far away from God? What steps are you going to do to change this?

FOR A GOOD FRIEND

It started off good, we started as every relationship would as friends hoping it would never end. Time and months passed and we grew more and more closer, and our bond was unbreakable, we felt the same and felt just alike but everyone else knew besides us.

Now, I didn't want to hurt him,
Nor does he ever want to hurt me.
I was his only true friend and as promised till the end. We fought, we cried, we laughed, we danced, we revealed our secrets with each other that we never told anyone else, it was us only and we didn't want anything to ruin it.

A year passed; calls were less
I knew something was wrong
My best friend has Cancer what could have gone wrong
He wrote in a journal and he told me to not read it yet for he knows his dying day is near and to not cry for he will be with me always.

I told him to promise me and remember to stay strong and to remember our phone calls that lasted all day long.

He was getting weaker and weaker
Cancer was controlling him
Changing him
He wasn't the same.

Until one day we had an argument and I told him please don't die
He said Please understand why
I didn't want to lose him, my only best friend. I'm here by your side till the very end of time.

We made up and hugs in the hospital bed
I try to keep my feelings inside from being oh so sad. I went home and felt something in me was torn apart. I knew it had to be him. I felt it deep in my heart. I got a phone call from his mother
telling me the bad news
Told me to go to the house, I have something for you. I arrived at the house with everyone there, everyone saying sorry for your loss. I made the speech telling the crowd about him. I couldn't help but cry and just wish he was here. It's not the same without him. I was on the verge of leaving. His mother stopped me and said, "Brendon wants you to have his journal and to read it and keep it for a lifetime."
I was honored and feeling happy knowing he gave me his journal inside was pages of when we first met, our fights and phone calls, and how he felt about me. And more of his secrets, I cried and said thank you B. For being such a good friend to me…

What is the true meaning of friendship to you?

What has each friend taught you?

Do you believe people are meant to come into our lives for a reason?

A MOTHER'S LOVE

A soul so kind, and so precious and so true

She is always there for you.

Every moment of every day, she always wants to make sure you're okay

You're her baby no matter what age,

Her constant need to love you and keep you close.

A love that is pure and radiant like an angel

She represents love and a love like no other

I am beyond blessed to have a woman like her for my mother.

.

Do you have a good relationship with your mother? What makes your mother special? Have you thanked your mother for all she has done?

What has your mother taught you? Any life lessons?

HAPPINESS PROJECT

Dear beautiful souls,

How are you all? I hope all is well. Life is full of surprises and when the Lord calls you for His glory, you just have to be obedient and listen to your heart.

It's been 2 years since I started a project called the **"*HAPPINESS PROJECT.*"** This project is to help teach others the importance of what it means to be kind, spread love, and encourage one another without hatred. I also made an Instagram page –> **dream_catcherx3: My Instagram page is all about quotes that I know will lift up the spirits of those who follow my page. This page is for the public so feel free to check it out, I'm open to opinions, and let me know what you think of it.** I also post quotes about God, inspiration, love, relationships, faith, hope, life, success, dreams, etc. I want to help people spread joy and goodness to those who need to hear it and to spread more kindness and love around the world. It is very important. In this world, I still believe that there is good in people.

I also made stickers and posted them around my neighborhood, the stickers say "you are a blessing to someone, every day is a day to be thankful, you are not a mistake, God is love" etc. I posted it all over; since it always breaks my heart to hear about all the negativity that goes on in the world nowadays. I say: "MORE LOVE AND LESS HATE!! LET'S COME TOGETHER AS ONE AND PRAY FOR ONE ANOTHER AND HELP EACH OTHER. IT IS FREE TO BE KIND TO SOMEONE. SO, LET'S START BY BEING KIND AND GIVE WHOLEHEARTEDLY!"

Do you want to help with my Happiness Project?

Sure!

(Please do your part to like and share, talk about it with family and friends, the world needs more goodness. Be the change you want to see in the world, it all starts with you!)

Being kind to strangers in the street, if you see someone in need, or a homeless person, help them and don't hesitate. Just listen to your inner voice. Follow your heart. Follow your intuition. We are God's people, and we need to serve others. It can be a small gesture or a simple text to someone you know who needs some uplifting. Helping out your community, helping an elderly in need, visiting a nursing home, or just buy something for someone you love. Family or a friend without wanting anything back in return. Knowing that you made a kind and genuine gesture, and it came from your heart. It makes you feel good knowing that you made a person smile and that you are changing their life for the better.

BE INSPIRED, BE MOTIVATED, BE DIFFERENT, BE YOU AND HELP ONE ANOTHER! ☺

How can we spread more love and joy to the world? How can we impact someone's life?

What are you doing for your community today?

What are you doing today that will get you one step closer to your goals?

What are your short-term goals?

What are your long-term goals?

Are you a highly sensitive person? Why or why not? And if so, you are still awesome!

What does being an empath mean to you? What is your soul trying to say? I am an empath and I feel everything so strongly. I now understand that the Lord made me like this for a reason.

BEING LOVED

You are loved.

You are loved in every way possible!

You are loved for your heart, for the smile you have

You are loved for what you believe in and what you stand up for.

You are loved wholeheartedly. You matter. Your feelings matter. Your thoughts matter. Your future matters.

So please remember, when you are feeling down when times get rough, and you feel like there's no way out.

Remember you are loved.

When people judge you by the way you live your life, and how you think differently.

Please always know you are deeply and truly loved.

You are loved even when you make mistakes. Remember darling we are all human and we are not perfect, with each passing day we learn, and we grow, but sometimes we get lost in our own thoughts.

And we forget that we are loved. Those thoughts that are not our own come to us and make us feel bitter in our hearts.

And we sometimes let that feeling overcome us and forget who loved us.

I'm here to tell you.

You are not alone. You are a beautiful soul with so much potential. Ready to be discovered.

The world needs more of your light. More of your gifts. More of your kind heart.

Sometimes we feel even though we live here, we are not from here. It's like we don't blend well with everyone. It is because we were born to stand out from the rest. Be an original. A pure jewel. A precious gem.

Those who know all about you will still love you and accept you for you. You just have to find the right people, find your unique tribe. Find the lovely souls who are like-minded like you, who have the same gifts as you, who love like you. And who knows you may learn from each other, but never forget one thing above all: learn to love yourself. Love deeply even if you get hurt ten thousand times, don't let it make you bitter.

Let it continue to make you walk strongly in love, the right person will appreciate all the love you have to give. Your love is precious. Let it naturally flow through your veins and be part of your daily ritual. Love conquerors all.

How can we change the world by showing more love to others?

What will you do this week to show acts of kindness towards others?

Who are the people in your life that show you kindness, what do you learn from them?

When someone treats you with kindness, how does it make you feel? Was there a scenario that happened in your life which made you change your point of view on people in our society?

What does the Bible say about Kindness?

Ephesians 4:32(NIV)

Be kind to one another, tenderhearted, forgiving one another, as God in Christ forgave you.

Luke 6:35(NIV)

But love your enemies, and do good, and lend, expecting nothing in return, and your reward will be great, and you will be sons of the Most High, for he is kind to the ungrateful and the evil.

Proverbs 11:17(ESV)

A man who is kind benefits himself, but a cruel man hurts himself.

Colossians 3:12(ESV)

Put on then, as God's chosen ones, holy and beloved, compassionate hearts, kindness, humility, meekness, and patience,

Proverbs 31:26(ESV)

She opens her mouth with wisdom, and the teaching of kindness is on her tongue.

RELATIONSHIPS
(Never give up on someone you love)

Have you ever thought about who has made such a huge impact in your life? Like something about this special someone has changed you from within and you've changed for the better. They have watched you grow and blossom into the person you are today. Do you value that person? Do you value that friendship? Do you value the person with whom you're in a relationship with? Can you think of that one thing that makes them unique from everyone else? How has this friendship or relationship changed you for the better or for the worse? Sometimes, we put all our time and effort into this one person, and little do we know the pain that is waiting for us in the end. We then question ourselves, "What did I do wrong, why did they do this to me?". Sometimes we out-grow them and they weren't meant to walk alongside us toward our destination. Think of it as; with each person that enters your life, they are either there for a season, a reason, to teach us a lesson. They are either here to stay for a lifetime or just part of the season we are in, of our lives. You know who this person is, just pray and it will be revealed to you. Are you being truthful and honest about your feelings? Always, express how you feel about someone. Sometimes feelings go unexpressed, and we regret not saying how we feel within that moment. You don't want to live life with regrets and then later down the line you look back and question, What if?

Always express your love daily to those you love. Appreciate them, cherish them, respect them.

Do everything with so much love in your heart that you would never want to do it any other way...
What if... we can live in such a way that only responds to love?
What if.... we can live in such a way that is not judgmental?
What if… we didn't listen to our inner critic, and we had less fear of the future?
What if... we sprinkle kindness like confetti and smile at one another?
What if...we follow our heart? and express gratitude daily?
What if... we come together as one and be there for one another?

How can you express love to yourself and others daily? One act of love is beautiful. Be that beautiful soul thinking of others, before yourself.

What does every relationship need? Is God in the center?

"Faith hope and love but the greatest of these is LOVE." 1 Corinthians 13(NIV)

What are your favorite love verses in the Bible? And what does it mean to you?

What do you think each relationship should have so it can flourish?

What are the qualities that you look for in a relationship?

Where can you find in the Bible where it explains what love is? Verse?

How do you express love to the people that you care about in life?

Is there someone in your life who you wish you can tell them how much you love them one more time? If so, who? Why? How does the thought of them make you feel?

Write your own poem here:

What the Bible says about showing Love to others?

John 13:34(KJV)
A new commandment I give to you, that you love one another: just as I have loved you, you also are to love one another.

1 John 4:19-21(NIV)
We love because he first loved us. If anyone says, "I love God," and hates his brother, he is a liar; for he who does not love his brother whom he has seen cannot love God whom he has not seen. And this commandment we have from him: whoever loves God must also love his brother.

1 John 4:11(KJV)
Beloved, if God so loved us, we also ought to love one another.

Philippians 2:3-4(NIV)
Do nothing from rivalry or conceit, but in humility count others more significant than yourselves. Let each of you look not only to his own interests, but also to the interests of others.

1 John 4:7-21(KJV)
Beloved, let us love one another, for love is from God, and whoever loves has been born of God and knows God.

Anyone who does not love does not know God, because God is love. In this the love of God was made manifest among us, that God sent his only Son into the world, so that we might live through him. In this is love, not that we have loved God but that he loved us and sent his Son to be the propitiation for our sins. Beloved, if God so loved us, we also ought to love one another.

Which Bible verse on love can you incorporate into your own life?

STRUGGLES OF LIFE

Have you ever asked yourself what is the purpose of having to go through struggles in life? Not everyone experiences the struggles of life the same way. Some are able to take the struggles of life and they are able to strive from it. Then there are those who falter from it. In the end, everyone's goal is still the same which is to overcome the struggles of life. For me, I am grateful for the good things that happened to me in my life and the bad. Some people may think, why? The bad situations that we go through in life teach us a lesson and make us wiser and stronger as a person. It is a blessing in disguise. What if we never go through any hardships in our life? Have you ever wondered to yourself "Will you be able to conquer anything that is thrown at you, or will you let the pressure break you?"? Always be thankful because in every storm there is a rainbow, it doesn't rain forever. There is always that light at the end of the tunnel. Never give up hope, lose faith, and never ever doubt yourself and keep pushing forward.

In your journal answer these questions:

What am I grateful for?

If I am feeling low, how do I cheer myself up?

Do I give up easily?

How is my relationship with God?

How do I react to positive feelings?

How do I react to negative feelings?

How do I cope with negative hardships?

Why is personal development important to me?

How am I feeling at the moment?

For 90 days (3 months) re-write and answer these questions to yourself. Make it a daily routine.

Are you taking time for your daily bread? (The Bible)

What do you value the most in life?

Have you ever seen someone for who they are, and they don't seem to see that of what you see in them?

SELF-LOVE: JOURNAL PROMPTS

More self-love and Less self-sabotage-how do you talk to yourself daily?

Why do we talk down to ourselves?

Why are we not accepting the person we see when we look in the mirror?

What makes you feel confident?

What is self-love? What does self-love mean to you, and how can we change our thoughts?

How can we love ourselves each day a little bit more?

Dear self,

Something I love about you is: _____

Today I am working on: _____

I am sorry for: _____

I love my: _____

My Flaws and imperfections make me feel:

_____
_____

Today's quote is: _____

Today's mantra is: _____

Today's affirmations are:

_____
_____
_____
_____
_____
_____
_____

I am a work in progress. And that is okay.
I am becoming the person I am meant to become.
Keep going!

Love, Me

_____

Dear self,

Today I allow myself to live in gratitude. How can I show gratitude daily?

The 5 things I am grateful for are:

1.

2.

3.

4.

5.

That peace that rests with my spirit.
(What makes me feel happy? _____ And the voice of hope that says all things are possible.

Love, Me

_____

(your signature here)

Dear self,

I am sorry for the negative thoughts of:

_____
_____
_____
_____

I am scared of:

I will work on myself daily to love myself more bydoing:

I appreciate you!

I love you!

I forgive you!

Love, Me

_____

What are my beliefs that are no longer serving me? For me was to let go of the pain from my past, the lord is in charge of my future. Now your turn!

What are your limiting beliefs?

When you write down all your beliefs that are no longer serving you, please get a new piece of paper and fold it in the middle. On one side are your old beliefs, and on the other side are your new beliefs that you have for yourself.

What are your new beliefs? (These new beliefs that you have for yourself will be part of your belief system and be part of your daily life). How will each belief benefit you?

In the Bible, it says: God is Love. How can you become a reflection of the Lord each day?

What are 5 insecurities about myself? How can I change them? Why do I have these insecurities?

What are ten things I love about myself?

1.

2.

3.

4.

5.

6.

7.

8.

9.

10.

Why do I love these 10 things about myself?

Am I being my truest, most genuine, authentic self?

I am most myself when I_____

How can you be engaged in the moment?

What does happiness mean to you? Where does it come from?

What are your favorite verses in the Bible that talk about happiness and hope?

What have you learned from your past experiences? Have they made you stronger or bitter?

The greatest gift that you can give to yourself is to learn who you are. Who are you? What makes you stand out? (Your hobbies, beliefs, looks, morals, background, family, culture, traditions, language, holidays celebrated, etc.).

Write nine self-love sayings about yourself that resonate with you. Example: I am beautiful. God is my strength.

1.

2.

3.

4.

5.

6.

7.

8.

9.

Look at what you've just written about yourself. (9 self-love sayings). Pick the one that resonates with you the most and write it on and post it. Put it somewhere you can see it, so you can always be reminded of how YOU'nique you are!

"YOU ARE WONDERFULLY FEARFULLY MADE BY GOD; HE DOESN'T MAKE MISTAKES!"

Psalms 149:14 (NKJV) "I praise you because I am fearfully and wonderfully made; your works are wonderful; I know that full well." What does this verse mean to you?
Write a letter to your younger self? What does he or she feel and what advice would you give her/him?

Write a letter to your future self. What will your future look like? Where would you live? What will your significance to others be like? Will you have a family? Will you have a car? **When you are finished, write on the envelope the year you would like to read it. You will be amazed at the transformation that you have made.**

Do you know God is concerned about what concerns you? (look into your Bible to verse Psalm 138:8(ESV)

Rewrite the verse.

What does family mean to you? The importance of family?

We all want to be remembered and leave a legacy behind, what do you want to be remembered for and why?

How do people describe you?

What has the previous year taught you?

What has Covid-19 taught you? What do you think God was trying to tell his people through this pandemic?

Have you ever taken a moment and took a step back to see how far you've become? How much did you accomplish? What has life blessed you with?

If you were able to go back in time and change one thing from your past, what would it be and why?

What makes you happy? Do you believe that happiness is an internal thing or external? Why or why not?

Describe a time in your life when the Lord had rescued you?

What is the Lord trying to teach you?

What made you smile today?

STORMS DON'T LAST FOREVER

Have you ever experienced depression, suicidal thoughts, or a survivor of a suicide attempt? Most of the time it is hard to talk about these topics, because we are scared of what people may say. But you are not alone. I've told you my testimony on going through spiritual warfare. How the Lord helped me, rescued me, broke my chains and I became a new creation in Christ. He has changed my life, and He lives forever in my heart, directing my path.

REFLECTION TIME!

Reflect on how you've changed in the past 5 to 10 years? What have you learned, and what is different about you? What have the people you grew up with taught you as a person? What do you hope to gain more of?

What are the areas in your life that you want to see a breakthrough in?

Who and what are the most wonderful places, art, movies, books, information, people, and things to you? And why, what makes them stand out from the rest?

What is your purpose? What sets your soul on fire? What are you passionate about?

Words and phrases to look inside the Bible:

Trusting God-verse says:

God knew you in your mother's womb verse:

What does the Bible say about "Joy"?

Verse on "GOD IS LOVE":

What does the Bible say when you are going through hard times?

God is our refuge and strength, an ever-present help in trouble ….

_____

_____

_____

(Psalm 46:1 (KJV):

Some Bible verses in trouble times:

The Lord is my light and my salvation; whom shall, I fear? The Lord is the stronghold of my life; of whom shallI be afraid?"
—*Psalm 27:1(KJV)*

"It is the Lord who goes before you. He will be with you;he will not leave you or forsake you. Do not fear or be dismayed." —*Deuteronomy 31:8(ESV)*

"Even though I walk through the valley of the shadow of death, I will fear no evil, for you are with me; your rod and your staff, they comfort me." —*Psalm 23:4(NIV)*

Have you ever questioned: "Where are you, God?". Have you ever felt lost, and the Lord led you home?

What is your favorite verse in the Bible and how can you relate it to your own life?

How can we live with humble hearts?

We all go through heartache. Someone who breaks our hearts, and we feel emotionally numb. What have you learned from your previous relationship that broke your heart? Do you still love them? Do you forgive them? Is there a part of you that still misses them, and why?

What is your favorite song to listen to that always lifts up your mood?

What do you need for self-development? In what areas of yourself would you like to change for the better and why? Has prayer helped you?

What is the true meaning of life? What have you learned about yourself through life's trials, challenges, and obstacles?

EVERYONE DESERVES TO BE LOVED

You are not too much or too hard to love. You are enough for the right person to love you and accept you for who you are. Someone who will love all your flaws and imperfections. Someone who is not judgmental, but someone who is unique and rare. They'll love you just as much as you love them.

Do you believe in true love & finding your soulmate?

If not, what happened that changed your mind?

CELEBRATE

Celebrate your wins! There is so much to celebrate when it comes to our goals being accomplished. Simply being alive and counting your blessings. Have you thanked the Lord for all He has done for you?

What are you celebrating? No matter how big or small?

Who do you want to be? Who is this person, how is their mindset? What do you want to be more of?

Date: Self Reflection:

Here is your daily check-in: DO THIS EACH WEEK IN A SEPARATE JOURNAL.

My number one priority this week is: (Any goals you may have).

I want to do less:

What works well for me this week was:

I want to do more of:

This week I want to feel:

To feel this way, I will:

I will pray when:

How do you feel after you've prayed?

List your own personal core values below:

As we heal ourselves, we also heal the relationships that surround us. How can you train your thoughts from negative to positive? How do you block those unwanted thoughts?

Every person has an untold story that changes them. But do we know that our own stories can help someone else and be their own survival guide?

What is your story?

Date_____

Today I'm feeling
_____
_____
_____
_____

right now, and that's perfectly okay. All my feelings and emotions are true, and I am worthy regardless of how I might feel.

In this moment, the thing I really feel like I need is
_____
_____
_____
_____
_____
_____
_____
_____

(A self-soothing activity of your choice)(what will make you feel better)

It would mean more:
_____
_____
_____

_____
_____
_____
_____
_____
_____
_____

and less
_____
_____
_____
_____

I trust myself to do what feels right for me. And that's okay!

MY FEELINGS ARE VALID! (Repeat this 3 times)

Even if that means I need to:
_____
_____
_____
_____
_____

If I need someone, I can reach
_____
_____

I choose them because
_____
_____

The greatest thing anyone could do for me right now is
_____
_____
_____
_____
_____

I commit myself to see the best in who I am. I will not have a negative mindset, but I will re-frame my thoughts to think positive in the moment. I will make this a daily habit for myself.

I love myself because I am _____,
_____, _____

YOU GOT THIS!

What does your soul need?

How can you be mindful of your needs?

(Circle as many of what applies to you)

TIME ALONE, BOUNDARIES, A FRIENDLY CHAT
REST, EXERCISE, FUN, A TEXT MESSAGE,

NURTURE, HUG, LEARN SOMETHING NEW,
A LISTENING EAR, A LAUGH, FOOD, TEA,

SLEEP, SPEND TIME WITH OTHERS,
BALANCE, ROUTINE, SOME ME TIME

START A JOURNAL, START A CLUB, READ,
DANCE, BAKING, CALL MY MOM

CALL MY DAD, SPEND TIME WITH MY LOVE,
BRUNCH, SOME WINE TIME, SPA DAY,
A NIGHT OUT, TIME WITH GOD,
STAY GROUNDED, MAKING PRAYER A HABIT

ACCOUNTABILITY   NEW FRIENDS
A NEW JOB   GO ON VACATION

_____   _____

_____   _____

Have you tried new hobbies? Challenge yourself to do something new.

Intentional Thinking

Having a thought but not sure why it's there?

ASK YOURSELF ….

Is this true?

Why do I feel this way?

Do I want to allow myself to think about it?

Does it get me closer to what I want?

What thought can I choose instead?

OUR MIND IS VERY POWERFUL. YOU ARE IN CHARGE OF THE CHOICES YOU MAKE IN LIFE. YOUR ACTIONS PLAY A ROLE IN WHAT WILL HAPPENED NEXT.

    LIVE LIFE WITH NO REGRETS.

How can you make more time for yourself? What is holding you back from taking care of yourself?

What are the elements of Self-love? Self-care? Self-respect? Self-kindness? Self-growth? Self-exploration? And self-awareness? What does this mean to you?

Write some verses that stand out to you that talk about anxiety?

Write a scripture that brings you peace?

Write a letter to someone special in your life and what do you want to tell them?

WRITE A LETTER TO GOD

DEAR GOD,

What are you trying to let go of from your past, trauma, childhood? Do you see patterns in your habit? Has what you went through affected you as an adult, and why? How can you forgive them and be at peace with yourself and your past?

"Accept your past, embrace your present, plan for your future."

What does this quote mean to you?

Reminder: stop focusing on how stressed you are and remember how blessed you are! Did you count your blessings today? Have you spoken to God and tell him how blessed you are that he is there for you?

How can you accept life experiences, so you can live in the present?

Matthew 6:34 (ESV)
"Therefore, do not be anxious about tomorrow, for tomorrow will be anxious for itself. Sufficient for the day is its own trouble.

What are the 5 things you can tell yourself to lift up your spirit?

What is something you will do today that can make the world a better place?
An example for me: there is so much hate. I continue to spread love and kindness in the world.
 Now it's your turn!

Finish the sentence.

"Be still _____ know _____"

Verse (   )

How can you be the light to others in this dark world we live in?

Today, take some time to look back and reread some of the previous entries you wrote in this book. What do you see? Any patterns?

Are you surprised by what you wrote? How do you feel from then till now? Are you seeing things from a new perspective? Do you feel different? What is the Lord trying to tell you?

Make a list of 30 things that make you smile.

Describe how the Lord changed your life?

What are some ways you can describe the Lord? What are the words that come to mind when you think of him?

I couldn't imagine living without…?

Make a list of the people in your life who genuinely support you, and who you can genuinely trust. Then make time to hang out with them, if you are unable to spend time with them give them a call, send them a card, or a text message.

Are there people in your life that you need to detox yourself from? Who are they, and why?

I really wish others knew this about me……

I really wish others knew I felt this when …

What are the qualities you look for in a partner?

Do you believe in marriage? Why or why not? Once you find that right person in your life, do you see yourself settling down and starting a family with them?

What is your definition of everlasting love?

Do you and your partner have a healthy relationship? How do you argue?

You can learn a lot about yourself from being with someone who loves you for who you are? What do you notice after being with this person? Are you happier? Expressing your feelings more?

What can you learn from your biggest mistake?

Make a list of what inspires you:

Each week be mindful of what the Lord has blessed you with…

How do you deal with anger? Do you have techniques that self-soothe you? What does the Bible say about anger?

What are three words that describe you?

What are your greatest attributes?

We live in a world where there is hurt, hatred, and discrimination. What is one thing you hope to change or can do daily to help our planet each day?

If the Lord was face to face with you, what would you say to him?

What is your definition of success?

Close your eyes and imagine the kind of world you would like to see. What is it like?

What do you think the Lord feels when he sees his children mistreat each other and the world?

What doubts do I currently have? How can I ease them? Why do I have these doubts? Did anyone doubt me in the past that made me feel this way?

What scares you about the future?

What will you do with your life if money wasn't an option?

What has this journal taught you about yourself? About love? About your life? About your mindset? About your love for God?

WHAT COMES TO MIND?

I am a human being that:

Loves to....

I want to...

Has morals that are ....

Has beliefs that are...

Has a goal to. . .

Has hobbies that are. . .

Is driven and inspired by. . .

Has habits and patterns of. . .

Gets mad when. . .

Favorite foods are...

Can self soothe by...

Believes in...

Will one day...

Who dreams of...

Who will travel to…

Favorite place to be in the world…

I wish…

I _____ PLEDGE TO BE

_____

_____

_____

_____

_____

_____

IN MY LIFE, I WANT TO BE MORE
_____
_____
_____
_____
_____
_____

I WILL PRAY
_____
_____
_____
_____
_____
_____

SO THAT I CAN WALK IN HIS FOOTSTEPS.

I WILL ACHIEVE _____
_____
_____
_____
_____
_____
_____
_____

I LOVE
_____
_____
_____

_____
_____
_____

ABOUT MYSELF.

I AM HAPPY. I AM WHOLE. I AM UNIQUE AND I AM LOVED.
_____
_____
_____
_____
_____
_____
_____

I PLEDGE TO BE TRUE TO MYSELF AND TO OTHERS EACH DAY AND BY DOING THIS IT WILL HELP CHANGE THE WORLD ONE DAY AT A TIME.

I AM PROUD OF THE PERSON I AM BECOMING, I HAVE GONE THROUGH SO MUCH IN MY LIFE THAT HAS CHANGED ME FOR THE BETTER AND THAT IS OKAY. I WOULDN'T BE THE PERSON I AM NOW IF I HAVEN'T GONE THROUGH THOSE OBSTACLES IN MY LIFE SO I AM THANKFUL TO GOD FOR IT ALL.

YOUR NAME HERE

_____.

WOOHOO!
YOU'RE ON FIRE!

YOU DID IT, BEAUTIFUL SOUL! HOORAY!!

HOW DO YOU FEEL?

YOU ARE EVERYTHING GOD WANTS YOU TO BE!

LET THE LORD GUIDE YOUR FOOTSTEPS INTO BECOMING THE BEST VERSION OF YOU.

KEEP PRAYING AND STAY IN FAITH & <u>NEVER LOSE HOPE AND NEVER GIVE UP!!</u>

-FAITH & LOVE
KRYSTAL

NOTES

Write your own poem or a phrase /quote that you love. Things that the Lord has shown you.

YOU DID IT, BEAUTIFUL SOUL!

I am so proud of you!!

Always remember …

You are what you think you can achieve.

God loves you!

You are on the right path!

To your success and Future!

You can do anything you put your mind to!

With Love
xoxo
Krystal

        " LET ALL YOU DO BE DONE IN LOVE"
           - 1 CORINTHIANS 16:14 (ESV)

www.ingramcontent.com/pod-product-compliance
Lightning Source LLC
Chambersburg PA
CBHW070901080526
44589CB00013B/1158